Grain

Grain is one of the most essential of all the world's resources. Without the enormous number of food products that are made from it, there would be more world-wide hunger than there is today. This book explains in detail how wheat and rice – the main grains – and also barley, oats, maize and rye, are grown, harvested, stored, transported, milled and made into foods and drinks. The history of grain, and its more unusual uses, are examined in the last two chapters. Alan Blackwood was an editor of children's books before becoming a freelance author. He has written many books for a variety of publishers, including *Focus on Tea* and *Focus on Sugar* in this series.

Focus on
GRAIN

Alan Blackwood

Focus on Resources series

Alternative Energy	Oil
Coal	Paper
Coffee	Plastics
Cotton	Rice
Dairy Produce	Rubber
Fruit	Seafood
Gas	Soya
Gold and Silver	Sugar
Grain	Tea
Iron and Steel	Timber
Meat	Water
Nuclear Fuel	Wool

Frontispiece *Grain crops have developed over thousands of years from various types of grass.*

First published in 1986 by
Wayland (Publishers) Ltd
61 Western Road, Hove
East Sussex BN3 1JD, England

© Copyright 1986 Wayland (Publishers) Ltd

Phototypeset by Kalligraphics Ltd, Redhill, Surrey
Printed in Italy by G. Canale & C.S.p.A., Turin
Bound in Great Britain at The Bath Press, Avon

British Library Cataloguing in Publication Data
Blackwood, Alan
    Focus on grain. – (Focus on resources)
    1. Grain – Juvenile literature
    I. Title   II. Series
    641.3'31   SB189

ISBN 0−85078−636−3

Contents

1. What makes grain?

A field of young wheat, barley or oats looks like blades of green grass on a lawn. As the crops grow, they become more like some of the tall wild grasses we see in the countryside. This, indeed, is what they are – special types of grass that have been developed and improved by thousands of years of farming. They are called grains, from the Latin *granum*, meaning 'seed'. Another name for them is cereals, from Ceres, the ancient Roman goddess of farming and agriculture.

Although they are types of grass, grains or cereals differ from other grasses in one important respect. Grasses on a lawn or the ones growing wild are 'perennials'. They produce a crop of seeds once a year, while the parent plant keeps growing from one year to the next. Grains, by contrast, are 'annuals'. The parent plant dies once it has produced its crop of seeds, so completing a yearly life-cycle.

Grains make up for this apparent weakness by providing their seeds with food, so giving the germ, or embryo, within each seed the best possible chance to germinate and grow – in much the same way that the embryo bird in its egg has food to help it grow and hatch. This is what makes grain crops so valuable to us. They grow much more quickly and easily than most other plant crops, and they yield grain seeds which are rich in food.

6

Left *These are some of the grains that you will read about in this book.*

Above *A wheat field in spring. Only the summer sun turns the wheat yellow.*

2. Grain as food

Wheat, barley, rice, oats, rye and maize (corn) are today's main grain, or cereal, crops around the world. Others are the varieties of grains called millets and sorghums, which are important food sources for both humans and cattle in parts of Africa and India. One type of sorghum is also used to make a sweet 'corn' syrup.

There are a few other crops that come close to being grains, though they are not technically classed as such. Buckwheat produces seeds that are widely used as a poultry and cattle feed, and can be made into a flour.

More wheat and rice are grown in the world than any other grains. This map shows where they grow.

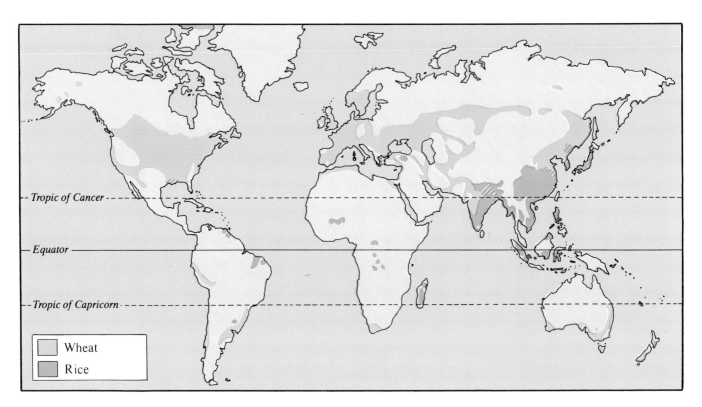

Grains belong to a large category of foods called carbohydrates – starchy substances made up of carbon and water. But they provide us with much else of food value. In varying amounts, the different grains contain protein, which the body needs to grow new tissue cells and stay strong. Some grains are rich in certain vitamins, which help the body to work well and fight off disease; in calcium, needed for strong

Grain is not only food for humans. It is also part of the diet of these Kenyan cattle.

bones and teeth; and in such minerals as iron, which enriches the blood and helps to keep us warm and fit in cold weather.

No wonder that grain gives us more food value for less cost and work than most other crops.

9

3. The wonderful seed

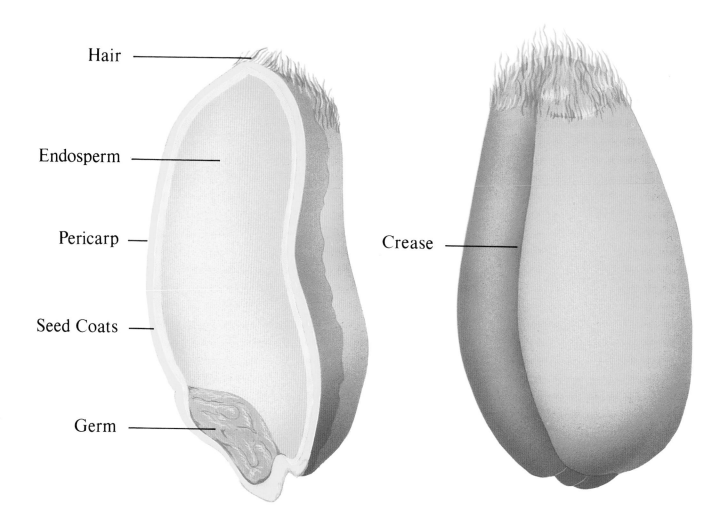

Hair

Endosperm

Pericarp

Seed Coats

Germ

Crease

Grains, along with other grasses, are self-fertilizing. Each plant contains both the pollen (male) and stigmas (female) needed to create a new crop of seeds. That is why grains and other grasses do not produce highly-coloured or scented flowers. They have no need to attract insects or birds to help them distribute their pollen.

The seeds of most grain crops form a thick, tight cluster called an 'ear' or 'head'. While still on the plant, they are covered by a coarse, leathery outer skin known as the 'husk'. The seeds themselves each have a thickish skin called the 'pericarp'. Inside are the two main parts of the seed. One is the 'germ' or 'embryo' – the actual part of the seed from which a new plant will grow. The other, much larger part of the seed is the 'endosperm'. This is the starchy store of food, on which the germ can live before the seed in the ground has grown its first tender roots and can take nourishment from the soil. The parent plant produces this by photosynthesis, the process by which all plants make for themselves starches and sugars by combining sunlight with carbon dioxide from the air and water from the soil.

It is from the endosperm part of the seed that we get most of the grain's food value.

Left *Grain seeds magnified to show their shape, and the inner parts of the seed. The germ is the beginning of the new plant.*

Right *A young ear. The swellings are the developing grain seeds.*

4. Wheat: the number one crop

At one time there were just two big wheat-growing regions: the Ukraine – 'the bread basket of Europe' – and the prairies of North America. Today, more wheat is grown around the world than any other food crop.

This huge expansion of wheat production is due to the work of botanists and other scientists. There are 14 basic species of wheat, but by the process of cross-fertilization (genetic breeding) hundreds of new varieties have been created, suited to cultivation in all sorts of conditions.

Above *New varieties of wheat and other grains are being developed and tested at this research station.*

Left *Sowing seed by hand.*

'Spring wheats', as their name suggests, are planted, or sown, in the spring, and grow and ripen in about 90 days (or a little under three months). Such varieties are ideal for the Canadian praires, where the summers, though hot, are fairly short.

'Winter wheats' are sown in the autumn and left to grow more slowly through the winter months, ripening from green to golden brown during the following summer. In Britain and other Western European countries, which have fairly mild climates, both 'spring' and 'winter' wheats can be grown.

The 'winter wheat' has just sprouted when autumn's crops are ready for harvest.

Yet other varieties of wheat now exist which will thrive even under the fierce summer sun of India.

All these wheat varieties bring with them another big bonus, for each makes a type of flour best suited for different kinds of bread, biscuit, cake or pastry. Consequently, wheat as a whole offers us a greater range of foodstuffs than any other grain.

13

5. Growing wheat

Though wheat, in all its varieties, is such a versatile crop, yields vary considerably around the world. The best crops yield about 30 times the weight of seeds planted.

Soil is an important success factor. Wheat needs a fairly fine and also fertile soil to grow well. Fertilizers and compost can help to achieve this. Many farmers also rotate wheat with such crops as potatoes, which help to keep the earth well broken up without taking too much goodness out of it. What wheat does not like is too much rain. Over 750 millimetres (30 inches) during the main growing period will spoil it.

For thousands of years wheat seed, like other grains, was sown, or 'broadcast', by hand – a very wasteful method. In 1733 Jethro Tull, an English agriculturalist, invented the first horse-drawn mechanical sower, which dropped the seeds into the newly-ploughed furrows. 'Fluid drilling' is the latest development. Seeds are first germinated, then placed in a sticky 'gel' that holds them ready for machine 'drilling' into the ground.

At harvest time, the wheat once used to be cut by hand and gathered in bunches, or sheaves, which were then stacked together into stooks and left standing in the fields to dry. After that it had to be threshed and winnowed – beaten in order to separate the grain from the stalks and husks then tossed in the wind so that the unwanted 'chaff' was blown away. Today, giant combine harvesters cut the crop, thresh it and deliver the grain, all in one operation.

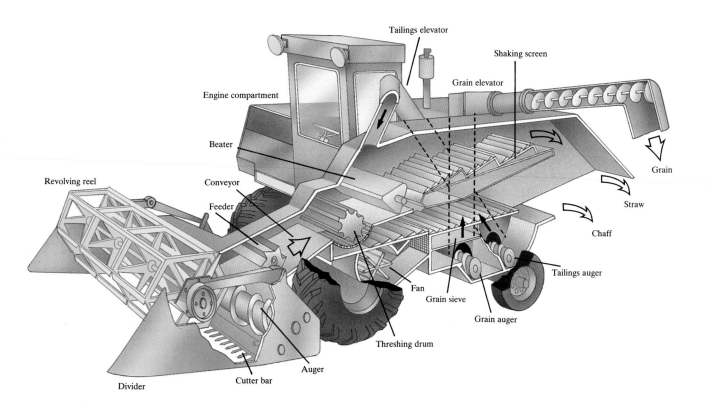

Tailings elevator

Shaking screen

Engine compartment

Grain elevator

Beater

Grain

Revolving reel

Conveyor

Straw

Feeder

Chaff

Tailings auger

Fan

Grain sieve

Grain auger

Threshing drum

Auger

Divider

Cutter bar

At the front of the combine harvester the crop is gathered and cut. The chaff and stalks are separated from the grain and dropped from the back. The grain is delivered from the side of the machine through the spiral elevator.

Left *Fields of wheat in West Germany.*

6. Rice: the great provider

The ancient Indian Sanskrit word for rice also meant 'sustainer of the human race'. For half the world's population, this statement is as true now as it ever was.

Rice is grown in many warm regions of the world: in parts of the USA and South America, in southern Europe and the Soviet Union, and in Africa. But 90 per cent of each year's crop is produced in the densely populated countries of southern Asia and the Far East. Unlike wheat and other grains, little of the rice is stored or left over for export. It is consumed in the countries where it is grown.

If you like curries and Chinese food, you will know of the biggest difference between rice and wheat. While nearly all wheat is turned into flour, most rice is simply extracted from the husk, cleaned (or 'polished') and eaten whole, boiled or fried. For hundreds of millions of people in south-east Asia, the daily bowl of rice – with perhaps just a little meat, fish or vegetables to flavour it – is their staple diet.

There are, unfortunately, big drawbacks to this way of eating rice. In the process of cleaning and polishing the rice grains (to make them look more appetizing), much of their protein and vitamin content is removed, leaving only the starchy carbohydrates. Many of those millions who depend on rice as their principal daily food suffer, therefore, from protein and vitamin deficiencies. 'Brown rice' – rice which has not been polished – is less attractive but more nutritious.

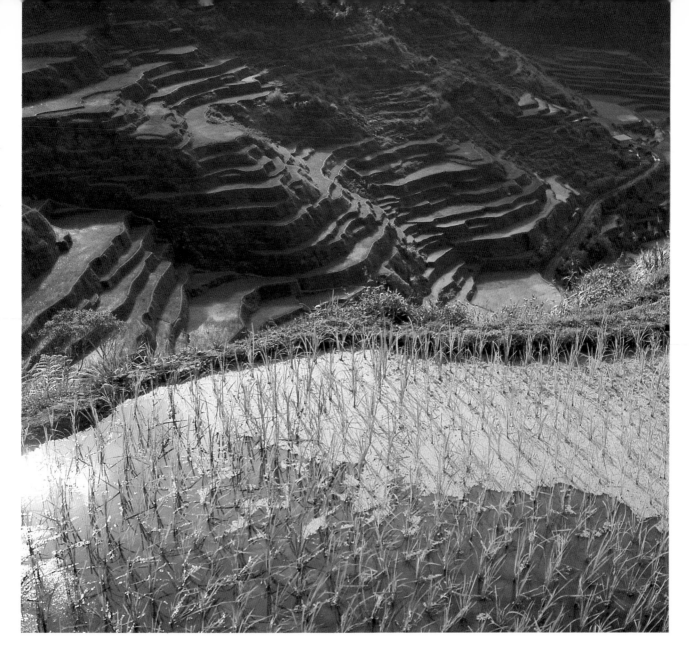

Left *This machine cleans and polishes rice. The unwanted husks come out on the left, the clean rice on the right.*

Above *Rice-fields must be flooded and therefore flat. In hilly areas, the problem is solved by these ingenious terraces.*

7. Growing rice

There are thousands of varieties of rice, producing grains suited to different kinds of cooking. But they are nearly all grown in the same way.

Wild rice once grew in tropical or sub-tropical swamps, and most of today's varieties are still grown in water. This makes cultivation a complicated business. The seeds are first germinated in a nursery, then re-planted in specially flooded fields (a field planted with rice is called a paddy field). The young plants should grow with only their tips above the water, which means that the water level has to be raised continually. This goes on until the rice has nearly reached its full height of about 2 metres (just

A Japanese farmer weeding a rice-field.

over 6 feet), and developed seeds. Then the water is drained so that the crop, now looking like other grains, can ripen in the hot sun.

In hilly country, the land has to be terraced, each small paddy field contained by banks of clay, mud and weeds, called 'bunds'.

Across south-east Asia, where most of the world's rice is grown, much depends on the monsoons, the seasonal heavy rains. If these come too early or too late, the crops are seriously at risk, and millions may go hungry.

When the time comes to harvest the rice, the water is drained away leaving the rice looking much like other grain crops.

New varieties are being developed, such as 'dry-land' rice, which can make cultivation much easier. But in India, China, and elsewhere in the Far East, rice-growing is a whole way of life, and the old methods, though they involve so much work, are slow to change.

8. Barley

Of all the grains, barley is the most like wheat. Both are grown over the same wide area of the world, and both grow to almost exactly the same height of around 90 centimetres (3 feet). One way to identify ripening barley is by the bristly spikelets attached to the seeds. These are about 10 centimetres (4 inches) long. A field of golden barley, its ears and spikelets nodding in a summer breeze, is a lovely sight.

There are two main species, or types of barley: six-rowed and two-rowed, according to the arrangement of the seeds on the ears. Farmers often grow barley and wheat at the same time, or in rotation. But barley, on the whole, is a tougher plant. It can flourish in lighter, thinner soils than wheat, because its roots do not strike so deep into the ground. It can also withstand colder weather (a quality known as 'winter-hardiness'), and can be grown quite high up on hills, where conditions would be too exposed for wheat.

Four or five hundred years ago, more barley than wheat was used to make bread and cakes. Today, very little barley is turned into flour. Much of it is grown as food for livestock, especially to fatten pigs; so that many of us may only consume barley indirectly, when we eat pork. With beer and whisky drinkers it is a different story. Barley, as we shall read in more detail on page 38, is the essential ingredient of these two famous alcoholic drinks.

This young barley plant is in flower; its short growing season makes it a popular grain.

Ripe barley is tempting food for a grub.

9. Maize (corn)

A maize field in England. The plants are large compared to barley or wheat.

People sometimes use the word corn to mean any grain or cereal. In fact, corn is just another name for maize.

Maize is the most distinctive of all the grains. As a plant it grows large, floppy leaves and a flower or tassel that sprouts from the top, while the grain seeds themselves grow from the stem in tightly packed bunches, or 'cobs'. Maize can also grow to a height of over 4 metres (13 feet). It is the true giant of all the grasses.

For thousands of years maize was grown by the North American Indians. The cobs of the original plants were not much bigger than a modern ear of wheat. Thanks to the kind of genetic breeding we have already mentioned, scientists have created varieties that now bear cobs ten times larger and more abundant than the ears of any other grain. Best known among these varieties are flour corn, sweet corn and popcorn (which gets its name from the fact that the seeds can be heated and 'popped' to make the well-known confectionary food).

One thing maize does still need during its three-month growing period is plenty of hot sun. It gets this in Australia, Africa, South America, the southern parts of Europe and the Soviet Union; and in the well-named American 'corn belt', which produces over half the total world crop. Much of all this is used as food for cattle and pigs, though the different varieties of maize produce a very wide range of foodstuffs, from corn oil to cornflakes.

Maize cobs litter the ground after this bumper harvest in Peru.

10. Oats and rye

Oats, which grows to a height of just over 1 metre (nearly 4 feet), is the prettiest of the grains. Its seeds do not form single ears or cobs, but hang in twos and threes from delicate little branches along the length of the stem. Varieties of the plant are distinguished both by the colour of the seed husks, which may be white, yellow or grey, and by the way the seeds and spikelets hang, in some cases all round the stem, and in others on one side only.

For all its delicate appearance, oats is a sturdy plant. It grows well in cool, wet regions, like Scotland, long famous for its oatmeal porridge. On the other side of the world, a lot of oats is grown in New Zealand.

Rye, which looks much more like barley or wheat, with bristly ears ripening to a brownish-green, can grow in even poorer conditions than oats. In the past it may have been regarded only as a weed, or at any rate as a poor relation of wheat and barley. Then, in those areas of Europe with a cool climate and rather poor, sandy or marshy soil – as in parts of north Germany, Poland and the Soviet Union – its tough growing qualities were appreciated. Rye bread, baked from the heavy, dark flour, is still a speciality of those countries.

Oats is a sturdy crop despite its delicate appearance.

Rye is one of the hardiest of the grains. The seeds are much smaller and closer together than on wheat or barley ears.

11. Storing grain

Many countries regularly produce a surplus of grain, which has to be stored. The grain first needs to be dried – or, to be more precise, to have its moisture content reduced to around 15 per cent of the whole. Grain that is stored too wet will rot, or be ruined by fungi and moulds. What is called spontaneous combustion is an even more alarming risk. Wet grain kept in store can start a kind of fermentation process that builds up more and more heat until it suddenly catches fire.

Grain is stored in special containers called silos. Some of the largest grain silos are in North America. Built of metal and concrete – to keep out rats, mice and beetles – they can each hold up to 300 tonnes of grain. Rows of them, rising up like skyscrapers, stand out for miles in the flat prairie lands where the grain is grown; and they tower above the big ships that make their way up the St Lawrence River and into the Great Lakes, to load up with grain for export.

Flour, whose manufacture is described in the next chapter, must also be stored at just the right temperature and at a controlled level of humidity, otherwise it will go mouldy. There was a famous – extremely rare – case in France earlier this century, when a very dangerous type of mould, called ergot, got into some sacks of flour. Some of the people who ate the bread baked from this flour went mad.

Silos for storing grain on the pampas in Argentina.

Unloading wheat by elevator into a bin after harvesting.

12. Milling

In the past people named Miller were sometimes called 'Dusty' by their friends. This is a reminder of the miller's job – grinding down seed grain into fine, powdery flour. Any grain can be turned into flour, but today most of the world's flour comes from wheat.

Milling is an ancient craft. Originally it was done by hand, grinding down the grains between two flat stones. Every part of the grain, including the tough skin (the 'pericarp'), ended up in the flour, which was of a coarse, uneven quality, more suitable for boiling up into a kind

Milling by hand in the Sahara desert. The grain is ground between flat stones.

The main picture shows the inside of a modern mill. Upper inset: how a modern milling machine works. Lower inset: close-up of milling rollers, with five wheat grains.

of porridge than for baking.

Gradually millstones were improved, turning against each other at different angles and speeds, so that the pericarp was removed from the other parts of the grain. Bullocks or other working animals were used to turn the millstones round. Then came water-mills and windmills, harnessing the power from swiftly flowing streams, or from the wind, to set the massive stones in motion.

Today milling is a highly technical process, involving more than 40 stages. There is not much dust about in a modern mill, although the machinery can reduce each single grain to as many as 20,000 particles of the finest flour.

A large modern mill also produces several kinds of flour. The most common sort is pure white flour, made by extracting both the pericarp and the oily, yellowish germ, so that only the starchy white endosperm is left. Wholemeal flour, on the other hand, includes the whole grain and is therefore more nutritious.

29

13. Bread: 'the staff of life'

In the Bible, bread is called 'the staff of life' – one of the most ancient foods and still a basic part of most people's diet.

You can make a very simple kind of bread just by baking a mix of flour and water, plus a little salt. The Indian chapati and the Mexican tortilla (made from maize flour) are examples of this flat or 'unleavened' bread, similar to pancakes.

The bread most of us eat, however, is 'leavened' by the addition of yeast. This makes the mix, or dough, rise and take on the familiar appearance and texture of a loaf when it is baked in the oven. The important thing is for the yeast to start fermenting before the dough is baked. At one time, bakers had to knead and pummel the heavy dough to make the yeast

Home-made bread on a Portuguese market stall.

Freshly baked loaves in a modern bakery.

start fermenting, or 'working' as they called it. In a modern bakery, machines like very large cake mixers prepare the yeasty dough for the oven in a few minutes.

Some people enjoy the thick, dark bread made from rye; but it is wheat flour that provides us with most of our bread. A big proportion of this is white bread, made, of course, from refined white flour. This lacks the protein and vitamins found in the whole grain, but in many countries there are laws which require these constituents to be returned to the flour before it is used to make bread, so that all types of bread have much the same high nutritional content. Nevertheless, health experts point out that since wholemeal loaves (the best type of brown bread) have a higher 'fibre' content, they are better for our digestion.

14. Biscuits, cakes and puddings

A glance in the window of a baker's shop or along the shelves of a supermarket will show us how much can be done with grain flour.

We can start with doughnuts, dough which has been sweetened and fried.

Then there are all the biscuits. The word comes from the Latin meaning 'twice cooked or baked', which was the old way of hardening and crisping up unleavened bread so that it would keep longer without going mouldy. Back in the days of sail, biscuits were an important part of a ship's rations for this very reason. Oatmeal biscuits or cakes are probably the closest we now get to this traditional product.

Today the range of biscuits is enormous and includes the crisp, unsweetened cream and cheese crackers; digestives; crunchy gingernuts; and such quaintly named delicacies as

Ginger biscuits in the making, before going into the oven.

garibaldis — a kind of biscuit fruit sandwich.

The choice of cakes and buns is just as wide, ranging from the lightest and fluffiest of sponge confections to sweet, crumbly shortcake and rich, dark fruit cakes.

Puddings and dumplings come in an even greater variety of forms. Flour is still the basic ingredient of the celebrated Christmas pudding, and of dumplings, which can either be savoury or sweet. Rice and semolina puddings, on the other hand, are made from whole grains. Different again are some of the meat puddings. The famous Scottish haggis is a mixture of meat and oatmeal (a coarse kind of flour), traditionally cooked in a sheep's stomach. The Scots themselves often have a glass or two of whisky (also made from grain) before they tuck into the steaming haggis.

Grain is the basic ingredient of all these delicious breads, cakes and pastries.

15. Pastry and pasta

Pastry is nothing more than baked flour paste. Yet this simple recipe provides the basis for such widely contrasting foods as delicate cream puffs and hearty steak and kidney or plum pie. The Italian pizza, now so popular as a convenience food, is also a sort of pie, with no top half to it.

Pasta is Italy's characteristic form of pastry. Pastas are made from a type of wheat (durum wheat) especially rich in gluten – a sticky, rubbery form of grain protein. The wheat is first reduced to a coarse flour or meal (semolina),

then turned into a paste and finally prepared in its various forms by feeding it through perforated plates or stretching it out and cutting it up. Pasta may also be prepared with a little spinach, beetroot or egg yolk added, which turns it green, red or bright yellow.

Pastas were once the mainstay of poor country people who needed to make a little meat, cheese or vegetables go a long way. They

The base of an Italian pizza is made from durum wheat.

were intended to soak up gravy, hold a sauce, or add substance to soup. Today, pasta dishes are popular with nearly everyone. Macaroni comes in the form of little sections of tube. Spaghetti means 'little string', which is a perfect description of how it looks when cooked. Vermicelli, thinner still, means 'little worms'. Lasagne and tagliatelle, by contrast, come in sheets, strips or ribbons. Yet another form of pasta is farfalloni (meaning 'butterflies').

Some of the many varieties of pasta.

16. Breakfast foods

The most famous traditional breakfast food is porridge, a word that comes from the French *potage*, meaning a soup. Porridge is a kind of thick soup made from oatmeal or some other grain. Another old cereal dish, now largely forgotten, was 'frumenty', made from wheat grains boiled up into a broth, enriched with milk, eggs, nuts and spices.

Porridge itself is still a popular breakfast food, but for a long time now it has faced strong competition from what are widely known as breakfast cereals – cornflakes, puffed wheat, and other 'instant' or 'convenience' foods.

This whole new world of grain foods was started back in the last century by John Kellogg, an American doctor who belonged to a group of vegetarians. He invented them to add variety to the group's diet. Afterwards his brother William started making and selling them commercially. Kellogg's is still one of the biggest names in the business.

Kellogg's original breakfast food was wheat or corn (maize) flakes. These are made by roasting the grains, rolling them out into huge flat flakes, and cutting them into small pieces. They are given a final toasting to crisp them up.

Pinipig, made from rice, is the Philippines' traditional breakfast food.

A Weetabix-type cereal being made.

The other basic breakfast cereal is puffed wheat. Here the grains are put in a 'puffing gun'. Under a combination of heat and air pressure they swell up and break open.

Today, other breakfast cereals are made from, or include, bran. This is the husks of wheat and other grains, removed from them by milling. Bran provides good 'roughage' in our diet.

17. Beer and spirits

'Liquid bread' was how brewers used to advertise their beer, to try and persuade their customers how good it was for them. The ingredients of bread and beer – grain and yeast – are indeed the same: it is the way they are treated that makes all the difference.

Barley is the grain used, and the first stage in beer making is to change the barley grains into malt – that is, to moisten and warm them so that they will germinate and start to sprout. By so doing they convert much of their own starchy food store into sugar. This process is halted by quick drying. The malted barley is then crushed and mixed with hot water, which dissolves the sugars, and forms a liquor called 'wort'. Hops (a bitter-tasting fruit) are added to give the beer its distinctive taste. Then comes the yeast, which completes the brewing process by fermenting and converting much of the sugary wort into alcohol.

Whisky ('the water of life') is a kind of distilled beer. The fermented wort is boiled so that the alcohol is first vaporized, then cooled and condensed, to produce the spirit drink best known as Scotch whisky.

Barley is not the only grain used to make spirits. Irish whiskey (spelt with an 'e') can be made with oats and rye as well as barley. Then

At a whisky distillery in Scotland.

there is straight rye whiskey, and bourbon whiskey (an American speciality), distilled from a fermented mix of maize, rye and barley.

Fermented barley and rye are also distilled to make various types of gin, and vodka ('little

A long line of beer bottles waiting to be filled before leaving this Danish brewery.

water'); while fermented rice gives us a spirit liquor with the Japanese name of *sake*.

18. The long history of grain

The story of grain takes us right back to the Neolithic (New Stone Age) Revolution – about 10,000 years ago – when people first started to settle in one place and farm the land. It was an event of enormous importance to us all. Instead of having to hunt for food all the time, people could start to grow their own. This was the first big step towards civilization.

American Indians preparing to plant maize in the desert. A stick is used to make holes for the seeds.

Emmer, the earliest wheat (right), did not yield the fat grains you can see on the present-day wheat (left), but was richer in protein.

found in a cave in Mexico have been dated just as far back in time. Maize, as we have noted, was an essential commodity for the ancient civilizations of the Americas – the Incas, Mayas and Aztecs.

A few years ago, a fascinating experiment was carried out by certain archaeologists into farming methods of Iron Age Europe (about 300 BC). One of the crops they grew was a very early variety of grain, called Emmer wheat. The crop grew to an uneven height, making it difficult to harvest. But the grains themselves proved to have more protein in them than today's main wheat varieties.

There is plenty of evidence to show how important grain has been to everyone, from the earliest historical times. Archaeologists exploring the remains of a long-lost town near the Persian Gulf found some grains which they reckon are over 7,000 years old. Ancient Egyptian wall paintings depict the growing and harvesting of wheat or barley. And it was the Egyptians who first used yeast to make bread rise in the oven. Other archaeological evidence suggests that rice was grown in China and India 7,000 or 8,000 years ago. Remains of maize (corn) cobs

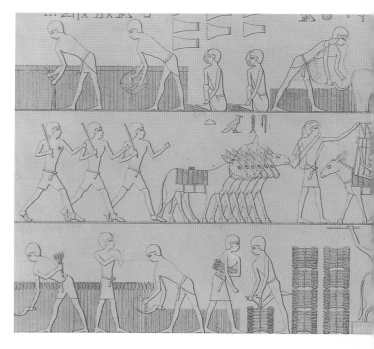

The ancient Egyptians used to depict their grain harvests.

41

19. Grain in world affairs

Grain has played a big and dramatic part in world affairs. One of the causes of the French Revolution in 1789 was the high price of bread, which brought millions of poor people close to starvation.

In Victorian Britain, the so-called Corn Laws of 1804 stopped the import of foreign grain, which kept prices high for local farmers and landowners at the expense of millions more

Emergency grain supplies like this one to Ethiopia are only temporary solutions to the problem of famine.

working people in the new industrial towns and cities. The repeal of these laws in 1846 was one of the stormiest chapters in political history. At other times and places, farmers sometimes burned their crops because they could not get a fair price for them, or because they could not sell them at all.

Today we are faced with other problems. The USA produces a huge surplus of grain each year. The countries of the Common Market (EEC) also produce far more grain than they need. Some of these surpluses can help to feed people in other parts of the world threatened with famine – grain being the easiest of foodstuffs to store, transport and use. In the long term, however, it would be far better for people in famine-hit areas to increase their own grain crops, with the aid of some of the new plant varieties and farming methods we have read about.

But grains are no longer only important as food. Their starches and sticky proteins can now be chemically converted for use in a host of other industries, from paper-making and textiles to cosmetics, glues and even explosives. It looks as though the future of grains is going to be just as eventful as their past.

Right   *The high price of bread was one of the causes of the French Revolution.*

Facts and figures

These charts show how much grain the world produces. Under each chart you can see which countries are included in the 'others' section.

Wheat

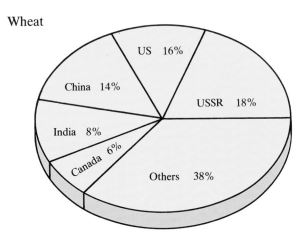

(France, Turkey, Argentina, Pakistan)

Rice

China 39%
India 17%
Indonesia 8%
Bangladesh 5%
Others 27%
Thailand 4%

(Burma, Vietnam, Japan, Brazil)

Maize

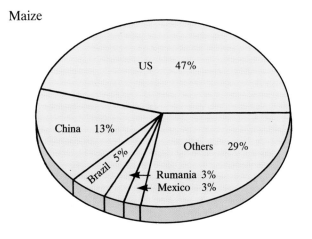

(USSR, Yugoslavia, France, Argentina)

Barley

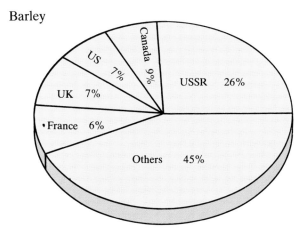

(West Germany, Turkey, Denmark, Spain)

Oats

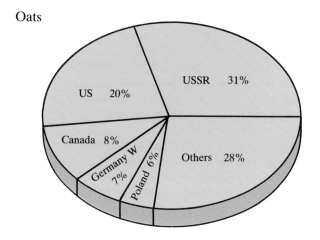

(France, Sweden, Finland, East Germany)

Rye

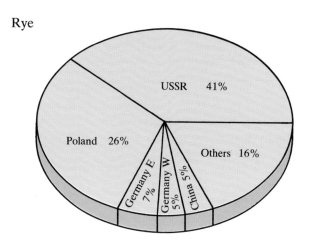

(Canada, Czechoslovakia, USA, Turkey)

Millet

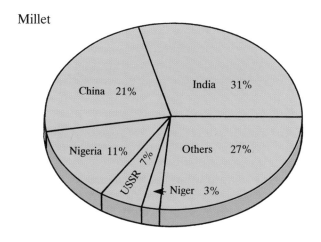

(Mali, Senegal, Egypt, Chad)

Sorghum

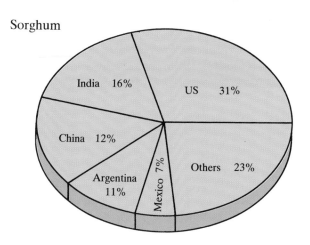

(Nigeria, Sudan, Australia, Upper Volta)

Glossary

Archaeology The study of prehistory to build up a picture of human life from relics and remains.

Bran The outer covering or husk of grains, usually removed by milling, but sometimes included in bread and breakfast cereals.

Carbohydrates These are foods consisting mainly of starches and sugar.

Chaff The husks of grain and other unwanted particles removed during harvesting or milling.

Compost or **Manure** Animal or vegetable waste matter that is 'broken down' or decomposed into chemical constituents like nitrogen and ammonia, which are good for the soil.

Crop rotation Changing the crops in a field so that the soil is not exhausted by the same crop each year.

Distilling Heating a liquid turns it to steam, which when it collects on a surface, condenses or becomes liquid again. This liquid, purer than the original liquid, is the distillate.

Ear The cluster of seeds that grow on wheat, barley and most other grains. Also called a head.

Fermentation The chemical process by which one substance is 'broken down' and recomposed as another. One type of fermentation changes sugar into alcohol, with the aid of yeast.

Fertilizer Factory-made compost (see above), including such compounds as ammonium nitrate, ammonium sulphate, potassium and phosphorus. This is different from fertilization (see **Genetic Breeding**).

Genetic breeding Fertilizing a plant of one variety with the pollen of another (cross-fertilization), to create a new plant.

Germ The heart of the grain seed, the part that germinates (see below). Also called the embryo.

Germination The first stage of growth of a new plant from the seed.

Gluten The protein substance, found in some grains more than others. It helps bread to rise and is also important in pasta.

Malt Barley, or other grain, that has changed its starch into sugar. Essential ingredient in the making of beer and whisky.

Meal A coarse type of flour, often made from oats.

Pericarp The skin covering of grain seed, not the same as the husk.

Photosynthesis The process by which plants make starchy substances by combining the energy from sunlight with carbon dioxide and water. From the Greek, meaning 'building from light'.

Pollen The powdery substance generated by plants for fertilization.

Protein Body-building food matter, essential for healthy cell tissue.

Semolina The hard grains, usually of wheat, left over after milling. Used in puddings and pasta.

Silo The large storage containers of grain or flour (from the old Greek word for a storage pit).

Smut One of the most common of the fungi or moulds that attack grain. It appears on ears of grain as little black smuts.

Starch Food material which is stored in plants.

Stigma The female part of a plant that is fertilized by pollen and produces seeds.

Terracing Sloping land is levelled into 'steps' or terraces in order to grow rice and other crops which need horizontal ground.

Threshing Beating harvested grain to separate the actual grain from the rest of the crop.

Vitamins Food matter that helps the body to function and to resist sickness and disease.

Winnowing The old method of separating grain from chaff (see above) by tossing it up into the wind so that the grain falls and the chaff, which is lighter, is blown away.

Books to read

EDLIN, H. *Man and Plants* (Aldus Books, 1967)
PEET, V. *Bakery* (Black, 1979)
RUTLAND, J. *A First Look at Bread*
  (Franklin Watts, 1972)
LUCAS, A. & J. *A Loaf of Bread* (Wayland, 1983)
GIBBS, R. *Maize* (Wayland, 1980)

Further information

For additional interesting facts and figures, especially about milling flour and baking bread, contact:

The Flour Advisory Bureau
21 Arlington Street
London SW1A 1RN

Picture acknowledgements

The author and publishers would like to thank the following for allowing their illustrations to be reproduced in this book: Camerapix Hutchison Library 9, 37, 42; Canada House Film Library *frontispiece*; 13 (R. Carr), 7, 30 (Eric Crichton), 27 (Nicholas Devore), 25 (Hans Reinhard), 24 (Leonard Lee Roe), 32 (Clive D. Woodley), and 11, all from Bruce Coleman Ltd.; Mary Evans Picture Library 43; Flour Advisory Bureau 28, 29, 31, 41 (left); The Mansell Collection 41 (right); Peter Newark's WESTERN AMERICANA 40; Picturepoint *cover*; South American Pictures 23; TOPHAM 20; Wayland Picture Library 6, 12 (left), 14, 18, 19, 22, 26, 33, 36, 38, 39; ZEFA 12 (right), 16, 17, 21, 35. The illustrations on pages 8, 10, 15, 44, 45 were provided by Malcolm S. Walker.

Index